STUDY GUIDE

WORSHIPER

HOW TO WORSHIP **WITH YOUR WHOLE LIFE**

BASED ON THE MOVIE

Hillsong

LET HOPE RISE

OUTREACH®

Worshiper: How to Worship with Your Whole Life Study Guide

Published by Outreach, Inc. Colorado Springs, CO 80919

www.Outreach.com

ISBN: 978-1-942-02725-6

Cover and Interior Design by Alexia Garaventa
Written by Jeremy Jones
Edited by Tia Smith

Printed in the United States of America

CONTENTS

HOW TO GET THE MOST FROM THIS GUIDE

Welcome to the *Worshiper: How to Worship with Your Whole Life Study Guide*, based on the film *Hillsong: Let Hope Rise*. If you have been to a church that sings modern worship music, you have most likely sung songs by the band Hillsong UNITED. Based at Hillsong Church in Sydney, Australia, the band has led millions of people around the world in worship. Their progressive worship music has topped music charts. The band has won many awards and been featured in major media coverage around the world. The recognition is nice, but as they like to say, "This isn't about us." What matters most to them is much higher.

"I believe God created music for the sole purpose of worshiping Him, to connect people, the human heart, our souls with heaven," says Joel Houston, the band's leader. "We're doing all this so one person somewhere who I might never meet gets to experience God in a new way and in a true way."

Joel and his bandmates love music. God has gifted them musically, and they are using those gifts to orient their own lives and others' lives back to God. They know the power of music can reach our souls and connect us with God's presence, but music is only one part of worship. Worship itself is expressing love, respect, reverence, and devotion, and we can worship with our whole lives. In fact, we are called to reflect love, honor, and glory back to our Creator in everything we do.

This five-week study will take you deeper into the ways of a worshiper and help you explore practical ways to worship through the ins and outs of daily life. Rooted in the film *Hillsong: Let Hope Rise*, you'll see how the band of worship leaders does that beyond the music and through the music. It's all about connecting with God in worship and being continually transformed by the process.

This study is primarily designed to be used by small groups or Sunday school classes. After all, there is power in worshiping together. But it can also be used by individuals for personal study and reflection.

Each of the five chapters in this book helps readers explore the purpose and power of, as well as the benefits of, plugging into God's rhythms of worship. Each lesson includes these elements:

KEY SCRIPTURE

A primary Bible passage sets the tone and theme of that weekly lesson.

VIDEO CLIP

A short clip from the film *Hillsong: Let Hope Rise* will share part of the band members' stories and offer a glimpse of worship in their everyday lives.

STUDY

This is your chance to dig deeper into the theme, sometimes with additional Scriptures, hopefully always with encouragement and inspiration. This section explores the deeper context and meaning, points to the Bible and draws out its guidance, raises questions, and sets the stage for discussion and application. You'll find it most helpful to read this part of the lesson before your small group meeting. As you do, mark up the text; write in the margins. Jot your own questions or ideas to follow up on in your own life and when you meet with your group.

APPLY

These suggested action steps are meant to generate discussion and offer suggested application. But they are only a beginning. Start with these ideas, and modify them as you follow God's guidance. And by all means, add your own steps to live out each particular area of worship. Each person's circumstances will be different. You might have the best idea yet.

DISCUSS

These thoughtful questions are central to the small group study. This is the time where members personalize the material and application points. And discussing responses offers greater breadth and depth of application for all. Just remember to speak and listen respectfully to all members in your group even if you don't necessarily agree with someone else's perspective.

SING

There is power in song, especially when sung together. Each week includes the lyrics of one Hillsong UNITED song. There's a good chance most of your group will already know these popular tunes. You can either sing them a cappella or sing along to the recorded versions. Your group might even want to close out your time together by singing several worship choruses.

We hope you will come away from this study with a deeper love for God and a broader understanding of worship. To be a follower of Jesus is to be a worshiper. Even in areas of life we might not immediately connect with worship, we can direct our focus and love to God, connect deeply with Him, and be transformed as we make worship a way of life.

WEEK 1

WORSHIP THROUGH FAITH

KEY SCRIPTURE

"Faith is the confidence that what we hope for will actually happen; it gives us assurance about things we cannot see." —Hebrews 11:1, NLT

VIDEO CLIP

Watch the clip for week 1, "Worship Through Faith," where Taya Smith shares her story of stepping out in faith.

STUDY

Taya Smith sat at a crossroads. You just heard her story. She was down to $200 and not sure what to do. But she did know where to turn—or Who to turn to. "All I said to [God] is that I wanted to sing and that I wanted Him to use me," she says. As for that next step, Taya would have to exercise her faith.

Have you ever been at a similar crossroads? Have you ever wondered which way to go? What to do? Have you ever asked God to use you—or wondered if He really could? You're not alone.

We humans are notoriously shortsighted, but we sure wish we could see and know the future. Our intentions are usually good. We want to serve God. We want to follow His will. We want to know what He wants us to do. But His ways of working that out are usually different from ours.

Often, we want Him to write a message in the sky or reveal a treasure map of sorts: *Go this way. Turn right at age twenty-three. Meet your spouse here. Head straight toward this city for a job offer that will lead you to a fulfilling career. Ask this person to mentor and disciple you. Have kids. Plug into this church. Take that mission trip. Volunteer in the other ministry. Stand strong and say no when your boss asks you to compromise, even when it costs you your job. Accept this position even for less pay; it will end up paying more and being far more satisfying than you can guess. Don't worry when that serious illness strikes your family; I'll heal your daughter/grandfather/spouse and use your story to encourage many other people. Love your kid when he rebels; he'll turn back to Me, and I'll use him in powerful ways. Spend more time with your family. You'll die at age eighty-eight, so build your spiritual and family legacy now. Then you and I will spend eternity together, and everything else will make complete sense.*

That sounds like it would be nice, but would it really be? Would we rest in the knowledge of how life will play out? Would we happily follow the script? Or would we end up trying to change the plans because we don't like them? Would we become bitter because we didn't get to choose? One thing is for certain: If God gave us a vision of the future, we wouldn't have any reason to use faith.

Someday we won't need faith. It's a vital thing here in this life, but it only belongs here on this earth. In heaven, when God has completed His final work, we won't need faith anymore. Everything will be clear. Nothing will separate us from God and our full trust and knowledge of Him.

But for now, faith is "the confidence that what we hope for will actually happen; it gives us assurance about things we cannot see" (Hebrews 11:1, NLT).

Faith is belief and action. Sometimes it glows like an ember; other times it roars like an inferno. God knows that the more we use it and fan its flames, the stronger it burns, filling us with hope and confidence—sometimes for a particular outcome in this life, always for the truth that our good God is taking care of us even when life isn't working out quite like we expected or prefer.

Choosing that kind of trust—choosing faith—is part of the way we worship God. We tend to think of worship as singing to God. It is, but it's more. Worship is the act of showing our devotion to God. It's opening ourselves to Him, connecting with Him, and letting Him shape us through the experience. Singing can do that powerfully but so can the process of putting our faith into practice.

When we seek God, pursue His counsel through people who are wise in His ways, and step out as best we can into the unknown, we show that we are willing to trust Him. We acknowledge that He is much bigger than we are. We demonstrate with our lives that we really are willing to follow Him. We show that we are willing to seek His face, not just His advice. We open ourselves up to encounter who He is, not just what He can give us.

And God uses that worship process to strengthen our faith and shape our character, to make us more of who He created us to be.

God has been working that way for centuries to shape His followers. The Bible is filled with examples.

PETER

Peter is a great example. The leap-and-then-look disciple was usually quick to voice his best intentions and leap into action. In Matthew 14, he was not only the first to step out of the fishing boat into a wind-tossed sea, he was the only one to get out of the boat when Jesus called. All the disciples were afraid when they saw Jesus strolling toward them over the waves. They thought He was a ghost. When Jesus spoke, maybe others believed it was Him, but only Peter believed it enough to do something about it. Only Peter stepped over the wooden railing when Jesus said, "Come" (Matthew 14:29).

We don't know how many steps Peter took on top of the water. The Bible doesn't say how far he made it—or how quickly the different thoughts and emotions flashed through his brain.

But we know that one second, wide-eyed Peter stared at his Lord and moved, defying gravity and all the laws of physics, but the next second he plunged into a chaotic sea when he looked around at all the reasons he shouldn't and couldn't be walking on water.

Sometimes the Bible is a little like e-mail: We don't quite get the tone and nuance of the original spoken word. It might be tempting to take Jesus's words to Peter as chastising: "'You of little faith,' he said, 'why did you doubt?'" (Matthew 14:31). But maybe they were delivered with more compassion and understanding, the kind a hopeful parent shows to a young child learning to ride a bike. Of course, that mom or dad wants to see the child succeed and ride happily down the street, but a parent knows there will come some crashes along the way. And a loving mom or dad will be there to scoop up that child with comfort and care. That's exactly what Jesus did. Immediately, Jesus reached out and caught Peter and carried him to safety.

Peter gave his best shot at faith. Fear got in his way. Still Jesus was there to catch him.

A FATHER

A father described in Mark 9 shows us another excellent example of the process of worshiping through faith. This man was at the end of his rope, desperate to find help for his son. The man described his son as possessed by a spirit that would throw the boy to the ground or into the fire or water, where he would seize and foam at the mouth. The affliction had plagued the boy his whole life. We don't know how many years it had been, but imagine the worry and fatigue those parents must have felt, every day watching and waiting on edge, wondering when and where they would have to spring into action to save their son's life. Maybe we would have recognized the illness as some form of epilepsy. They had no such medical knowledge. The only thing they and their family and community could attribute this awful condition to was an evil spirit. They must have felt shame. They would have questioned why. They certainly felt helpless. They would have been desperate. So the father came to Jesus for help.

It must have taken all the hope he could muster. He had heard the stories about Jesus's miracles. This man, the Messiah, had healed others—maybe He could heal their son. Was it too much to ask? Perhaps it seemed that way when Jesus's disciples failed to heal the boy.

"If you can do anything, take pity on us and help us," the father pleaded (Mark 9:22).

If? asked Jesus.

"If you can?" said Jesus. "Everything is possible for one who believes." Immediately the boy's father exclaimed, "I do believe; help me overcome my unbelief!" (Mark 9:23–24).

What a beautiful proclamation! This man had endured years of disappointment and shame. He had been bent low by the burden of helplessness. He wanted to believe. Maybe all he had was a tiny speck of hope deep within him, and that's what he brought to Jesus, crying out for help.

Uncertainty and rationality tried to get in the father's way. But the man stepped out on a limb of hope, not knowing what would happen. And Jesus caught him. He healed his son. That boy, that father, that family would never be the same.

HALL OF FAMERS

Hebrews 11 gives a whole list of people commended for their faith. Some aren't surprising; others are. One thing is for certain: None of those members of the Hall of Faith were perfect, and neither was their faith.

Take Abraham, for example. Abraham journeyed into the unknown but botched attempts to bring about God's promise through his own plans. Remember lying about his wife, Sarah, in Egypt and trying to bring about the promised child with Hagar? Abraham let impatience get in the way of his faith.

The fact that even the greats of the faith struggled and fell short is encouraging for the rest of us who struggle and doubt and want to believe but have trouble getting out of the boat or taking that uncertain step. Sometimes faith is trying to believe. It's reaching for and clinging to hope. Jesus meets us where we are—in our best effort, even if it's feeble.

When we take a step of faith, when we grab hold of belief and let it propel us into motion and action, we lift up God. We reflect glory to Him. We show our love and devotion to Him. We worship.

A BOY

Sometimes it doesn't take much. Maybe that was the case for the boy in the crowd in John 6 with some fish and bread. When the disciples asked, the boy trusted that Jesus and His followers would do good. Maybe the boy hoped for some kind of miracle. Maybe he just did what the grown-ups asked. Whatever was going through his mind, the boy offered what he had, small as it was. Jesus took his meager snack and made a large-scale miracle out of it.

Sounds like us a lot of the time—unsure what to do, feeling we have nothing but a simple prayer and the heart's desire for God to use us. Thankfully God meets us in just those situations and circumstances. We won't receive a full life plan, but we can receive the hope to take the next step and to faithfully lift up God. That's the faith of a worshiper.

APPLY

How can we worship through faith?

SEEK

In light of all the examples of faith in Hebrews 11, the next chapter urges us to follow their example. How? By "fixing our eyes on Jesus, the pioneer and perfecter of faith" (Hebrews 12:2). The principle is the same as driving a car or riding a bike—where you look is where you'll go. To deepen our understanding and trust of God, we have to focus on Him. What circumstances or uncertainty are we faced with? Turn toward Jesus. Dig into His Word. Ask for the counsel of people who are wise in His ways.

ACT

Second Corinthians 5:7 says, "For we walk by faith, not by sight" (ESV). Walking takes place step by step. As we align our focus and our lives with God's Word, we also need to take the next step before us. And in our forward motion, He meets us, and we can continue to reflect glory to Him along the way. What's your next step?

CHOOSE TO BELIEVE

Sometimes faith is easy. Sometimes faith is hard. Often, it requires a conscious choice to believe what we cannot see, what defies our feelings or circumstances. Sometimes it's crying out like the father in Mark, "Help me overcome my unbelief!" That kind of choice realigns our vision and purpose. It leads us to less of ourselves and more of God.

DISCUSS

Which of the Bible characters we've read about do you identify with most?

What struggles do people have with faith?

How has your faith been tested? What was the result?

How are you tempted to finish this sentence? I'm just a ___________________________. How do you think God wants to use you anyway?

What step of faith is God leading you toward?

SING

Worship and sing together. Stream the following song or Google the lyric video.

"BROKEN VESSELS (AMAZING GRACE)"

All these pieces
Broken and scattered
In mercy gathered
Mended and whole
Empty handed
But not forsaken
I've been set free
I've been set free

Amazing grace
How sweet the sound
That saved a wretch like me
I once was lost
But now I'm found
Was blind but now I see

Oh I can see it now
Oh I can see the love in Your eyes
Laying Yourself down
Raising up the broken to life

You take our failure

You take our weakness

You set Your treasure

In jars of clay

So take this heart, Lord

I'll be Your vessel

The world to see

Your love in me

[repeat chorus]

WEEK 2

WORSHIP THROUGH CALLING

KEY SCRIPTURE

"As a prisoner for the Lord, then, I urge you to live a life worthy of the calling you have received. Be completely humble and gentle; be patient, bearing with one another in love. Make every effort to keep the unity of the Spirit through the bond of peace. There is one body and one Spirit, just as you were called to one hope when you were called; one Lord, one faith, one baptism; one God and Father of all, who is over all and through all and in all." —Ephesians 4:1–6

VIDEO CLIP

Watch the clip for week 2, "Worship Through Calling," where Jad Gillies and Jonathan "JD" Douglass give glimpses into their families' lives and sacrifices.

STUDY

Have you ever dreamed of touring the country or the world? Do the big stage and bright lights sound appealing? Do you picture exotic locations and vibrant cities and adoring fans?

It's far less glamorous than you might think. The reality is long hours in a cramped bus or van, late-night departures or arrivals, the same old unhealthy road food, mile after interstate-mile where every exit and gas station look the same. Even the glare of spotlights can blur together on stage after stage.

Most traveling musicians will tell you that touring is a grind. The logistical slog of taking their art to fans is not the part that draws most musicians to the career. It's hard to wake up in a different city, country, or time zone every morning. It's even harder to be away from home and families—even when the purpose lies much deeper than simply making good music, as is the case for the members of Hillsong UNITED. As Jad

Gillies and Jonathan "JD" Douglass and their families know all too well, leading worship professionally is deeply fulfilling and meaningful, but it comes with very real challenges.

What makes it worthwhile for Jad and JD—and their wives and kids—when the hours away are long and the miles are far? What keeps these men going when they would rather stay? What keeps their wives staying when they would rather go with their husbands, or not be left to parent alone?

Calling.

Calling makes things worth it. Calling defines our purpose. It gives us a sense of mission. It draws us into God's higher ways. It keeps us going when the way is tough and the challenges are big.

"I believe God created music for the sole purpose of worshiping Him, to connect people, human heart, soul with heaven," says Hillsong UNITED leader Joel Houston. "We're doing all this so one person somewhere, who I may never meet, meets God in a new way, a true way."

For all the members of Hillsong UNITED, leading worship is a calling. But to live in God's calling in any area—not just music—is a form of worship. Doing so is an expression and affirmation of who God has made us to be and the gifts He has given us. Worshiping through our calling aligns us to God's purpose. It keeps us listening and tuning our ear to His voice. It's an expression of obedience and submission to our Heavenly Father. Worshiping through calling blends the use of our God-given gifts with new opportunities that stretch our faith and keep us depending on God's strength. In them, God is lifted up.

CLEAR AND SPECIFIC CALLING

As we discussed in the last lesson about faith, most of us want a clear road map—a specific calling—from God. We read about it in the Bible and think it sounds good. We want to be like

Moses and Paul. God had big plans for those two men. And He made sure they knew it. You know the stories.

Moses was roaming around herding sheep or goats in the desert for years. Maybe he really liked goats. Maybe he was happy with the job because it was the family business. One thing Moses must have liked about the job was that it was far from Egypt. After killing a man in Egypt years before, Moses was an outlaw—or you might say, just the kind of person God likes to use.

So in the middle of nowhere in the middle of Moses's incognito career, God showed up in a miraculous burning bush with a clear, unmistakable call: Go back to Egypt and tell Pharaoh, "Let My people go." Would you be excited to receive a call that clear from God? Moses most definitely was not. He did all he could to get out of it. He gave God all the excuses he could think of. He made his best case for why he was the worst pick for the job, including that he was a terrible speaker. God didn't disagree; He sent Moses's brother, Aaron, along to help. But still God said go.

The apostle Paul had a similarly famous miraculous encounter with God. Paul was enemy number one to the young Christian Church, persecuting, imprisoning, beating, and killing the followers of Jesus. In Acts 9, he was on his way to Damascus for a raid there when he ran into Jesus Himself—not Jesus in His earthly form but the heavenly, glorious Son of God. You could say Paul's experience was more of a wake-up call than a specific mission. The main message was to clarify that Jesus was God. His instructions to Paul, blind the whole time, were to go and wait in the city for further instructions. But Paul obeyed Jesus's call, and it transformed his life.

God used both Moses and Paul in mighty, life-changing ways. They were both fathers of the faith. They changed the destinies of the Jewish race and the Christian Church, respectively. Big tasks for sure—monumental ones. Maybe that's why God gave them big, clear calls.

Does God still do the same for us? He certainly can. And if God were to call you to change the destiny of His people, maybe He would make that mission miraculously clear.

GENERAL CALLING

On the other hand, God still can and does speak to us clearly, guiding us toward His ways and paths for our lives—and specific tasks—without necessarily blinding us along the road. Most often that happens by the guidance of His Holy Spirit confirming His written Word (John 14:26). Lots of times that process includes counsel and confirmation from wise Christians in our lives.

But there is a call that God has given all humanity: to know Him and to make Him known.

Let's look back at the beginning of everything. Adam and Eve—humanity—were created in God's image to care for all of creation (Genesis 2:15). They walked together with God through the garden and lived in perfect union with each other and with God. They knew God, and everything in the world was whole and as God intended. Of course, things didn't stay that way. Adam and Eve sinned. The world was broken. The barrier was built between God and His creation.

Then came Jesus to fix all that was damaged and to make things right between humans and God. The price was tremendous—His suffering and death beneath the burden of all the sins of every person throughout history, past and future. But the result was forgiveness and true, abundant, and eternal life—the life God originally designed in relationship with Him. With Jesus's work in securing it, He offered a call to every single person on earth for all time: Come and know true life with God (John 1:12; John 3:16; John 10:10).

This is the foundational calling for all of us: Come and be made whole in knowing God through Jesus. Even when we question what it looks like for us to live out that reality on earth, we can rest in the fact that we are created to know God and experience the gratitude, love, and security He fills us with.

When we remember and focus on that fact, we worship God by realigning our hearts and minds to Him and His purposes. We are renewed and restored and filled with fresh strength. It's then that we can fulfill the mission that Jesus has called all of His followers to: "Go and make disciples of all nations, baptizing them in the name of the Father and of the Son and of the Holy Spirit, and teaching them to obey everything I have commanded you" (Matthew 28:19–20).

THE CALLING OF GIFTS

Worshiping through calling leads us to live in ways that reflect glory to God and point to Jesus. Will that look the same for all of us? Absolutely not. It can happen in many ways and many forms. Each of us has unique gifts, abilities, and circles of influence through which we can touch other peoples' lives. Some of us will be on the stage—literally and figuratively. Some will be setting up the stage. Some will be at home. And others will be in a completely different arena.

As Paul wrote, "Just as a body, though one, has many parts, but all its many parts form one body, so it is with Christ" (1 Corinthians 12:12). Each of those parts is vital to the body.

> If the whole body were an eye, where would the sense of hearing be? If the whole body were an ear, where would the sense of smell be? But in fact God has placed the parts in the body, every one of them, just as he wanted them to be. If they were all one part, where would the body be? As it is, there are many parts, but one body. (1 Corinthians 12:17–20)

To embrace the abilities God has given us and to offer back those abilities for His use is a form of embracing our calling—

and worshiping through it. That's true no matter how important or insignificant our role might seem to us.

In *Hillsong: Let Hope Rise*, Lauren Douglass, JD's wife, says, "I've got maybe the less glamorous side of us; I'm not doing the tour. I am home with kids. But I remember growing up as a young Christian girl saying, 'God use me, whatever way, use me.' And this is the call [He's] put on both of our lives right now. I want to do that the best I can. I see my role at home as really vital."

A worshiper who understands calling keeps their eyes on God's bigger picture even on the difficult days and seeks to lift up God through the use of their gifts and in everyday life.

APPLY

How can we worship through calling?

KNOW YOUR FOUNDATION

Remember that the heart of any calling is to know God Himself. It's His first and foremost priority: to know and restore you and every other person in the world. He has designed and created you to know Him. Don't get so caught up in trying to find your calling to God's tasks that you miss finding God Himself. As you live in fellowship with Him, He will shape you, guide you, and use you naturally as part of His body (1 Corinthians 12:27).

USE YOUR GIFTS

God gave you gifts and abilities and passions. Using them as He intended reflects worship back to Him. Doing so pleases God's heart, and there's a good chance it resonates deep within your own heart as well. Pursuing those actions that make your heart come alive with a spirit of surrender can be an act of worship through calling.

REMEMBER WHY

Even when you are using your gifts, pursuing your passions, and following God's calling, there will be times when the way is hard and you wonder what you're doing and why. Refocusing on God's bigger vision can remind you. It can draw your attention to His bigger picture. It can help you recall a moment or milestone that set you on a particular path. It can renew your resolve and fill you with new strength. It can give you the hope and strength to carry on (Isaiah 40:31). It can fill your heart with worship and realign it to God Himself.

DISCUSS

How do you usually think of "calling"?

Was there a time God called you to a specific task or mission? What did that look like?

How have you felt discouraged about some aspect of your calling? How did you deal with it, or how are you dealing with it?

Who in the Bible received a specific calling from God? Was that an easy or difficult process for them?

How has God answered your prayers to be used—even unexpectedly?

SING

Worship and sing together. Stream the following song or Google the lyric video.

"NO OTHER NAME"

One name
Holds weight above them all
His fame
Outlasts the earth He formed
His praise
Resounds beyond the stars
And echoes in our hearts
The greatest One of all

His face
Shines brighter than the sun
His grace
As boundless as His love
He reigns
With healing in His wings
The King above all kings
The greatest One of all

Lift up our eyes, see the King has come
Light of the world reaching out for us
There is no other name
There is no other name
Jesus Christ our God

Seated on high, the undefeated One
Mountains bow down as we lift Him up
There is no other name
There is no other name
Jesus Christ our God
Jesus

Find hope
When all the world seems lost
Behold
The triumph of the cross
His power
Has trampled death and grave
Our life found in His name
The greatest name of all

Lift up our eyes, see the King has come
Light of the world reaching out for us
There is no other name
There is no other name
Jesus Christ our God

Seated on high, the undefeated One
Mountains bow down as we lift Him up
There is no other name
There is no other name
Jesus Christ our God
Jesus

The earth will shake
And tremble before Him
Chains will break
As heaven and earth sing
Holy is the name
Holy is the name of
Jesus, Jesus, Jesus
[repeat]

Lift up our eyes, see the King has come
Light of the world reaching out for us
There is no other name
There is no other name
Jesus Christ our God

Seated on high, the undefeated One
Mountains bow down as we lift Him up
There is no other name
There is no other name
There is no other name
There is no other name
Jesus

WEEK 3

WORSHIP THROUGH PAIN

KEY SCRIPTURE

"I have told you these things, so that in me you may have peace. In this world you will have trouble. But take heart! I have overcome the world." —John 16:33

VIDEO CLIP

Watch the clip for week 3, "Worship Through Pain," where the worship leaders reveal their pain and hard times and share how God has carried them through.

STUDY

What would you do? Matt Crocker and his family found his teenage sister dead. Michael and Naomi Chislett endured their infant son's open-heart surgery and heard the doctors tell them his odds of making it were not good. Brian Houston had to confront and hear his father confess that, yes, he had abused a child. How would you handle scenarios like those? How have you?

It's a fact of life we all hate: Pain is inevitable. Hard times will come. Their severity may vary, but difficulties and hardships will happen. There's no way to completely escape them on this broken earth.

Grappling with pain and suffering is an ancient problem. Those emotions entered the world with Adam and Eve's fall and have been a consistent part of life ever since. The Bible book of Job is probably the best-known example of trying to make sense of pain and suffering. Although we don't know the exact date it was written, we know it's an old book, even compared with other parts of the Bible.

You know the story of Job: Job is a good man. He's rich by every measure of his day: livestock, servants, children, the love of his family, and the respect of his community. Job is a leader and a patriarch. He is "the greatest man among all the people of the East" (Job 1:3), and he's living the good life. Job loves God wholeheartedly. In fact, God is proud of him and says so to Satan. Satan answers, "Duh, it's only because Job has it so good down there on earth. Let me at him, and Job will be cursing Your name." God—and here's the part in the story where we scream at the figurative screen, *Noooo! Don't do it!*—says okay.

So Satan lays waste to Job's life. He plunders his flocks and servants. He kills his children. He ravages Job's health. Imagine yourself in a complete personal apocalypse, and you get a taste of Job's experiences. Job's wife has enough. "Curse God and die!" she tells her husband (Job 2:9). But Job maintains his faith and trust in God. "Shall we accept good from God, and not trouble?" he tells his wife (Job 2:10).

That doesn't mean Job doesn't question. He grieves profoundly. He curses the day he was born and longs for death to find some relief. He also has to listen to his friends try to come up with answers for why things have gone so wrong. Their main theory is that Job must have done something wrong to deserve such pain. Job maintains his innocence, and he essentially pleads, "Why, God?"

Finally God shows up and speaks. He doesn't explain everything or wrap it up in a bow. But He proclaims His higher power and abilities far beyond humanity. It's not exactly the way we would like the story to go. We, like Job, want answers. We want reasons and explanations. We want everything to make sense. But Job reminds us that we won't always get them—that instead we can worship God through our pain. We can choose humility and acceptance and perhaps encounter God in ways that we wouldn't have been able to otherwise. "My ears had heard of you but now my eyes have seen you," Job says (Job 42:5).

WHY OR WHY NOT?

Jesus gives us another example of people trying to make sense of pain. Luke 13:1–5 tells us about some people trying to come up with explanations about why bad things happen. Their reasoning is that bad things must happen to bad people. Somehow the victims of tragic deaths must have brought it upon themselves because of some sin. Jesus says no. The Galileans they were talking about who were killed by Pilate were not being punished. Eighteen people who died when a tower collapsed on them weren't either. We all sin, and we all need God's forgiveness. But sometimes bad things just happen to good people.

The question is: When suffering touches our lives, how will we respond?

Why isn't necessarily a bad question to ask. It's a natural response. But it's important to remember that in the face of pain, we will rarely get the kind of answer we think we want to that question. Instead, it can be good to ask if there are choices we've made, actions we've taken to bring about the painful circumstances we're in. Obviously, that won't always be the case. Some tragedies or events are simply beyond our control; that's often true of illness or natural disaster. But there are times when our own unwise decisions lead us into painful consequences. Maybe that's the case with relational pain, for example.

Please hear this loud and clear: The point here is not to beat yourself up over mistakes you may have made; instead, it's to seek forgiveness and to learn from and grow through difficulty. In some cases, growing in wisdom may lead us away from a repeat of the pain we're experiencing. No matter what causes our suffering, we ultimately want our bitter or confused *Why?* to turn into an honest, prayerful, and humble *Why, God?* But we won't always get an answer this side of heaven.

GOD WITH US

What's most important to remember if and when your life takes a turn for the worse is that you are not alone. It's no coincidence that Jesus became human, came to earth, and walked and lived and existed as one of us—to feel our emotions and pain. It wasn't by mistake that Jesus was called "'Immanuel' (which means 'God with us')" (Matthew 1:23).

It might be tempting to think that when we give our lives to Christ, everything will be okay. But even Jesus told His followers that trouble will still come in this life on earth: "I have told you these things, so that in me you may have peace. In this world you will have trouble. But take heart! I have overcome the world" (John 16:33).

Jesus offers peace, encouragement, comfort, a bigger perspective—and His presence in the midst of our problems and pains. His Spirit is with us and in us no matter what we face, interceding for us when our grief is so great we have no words (Romans 8:26–27). His Word is packed with reminders that can fill us with unexplainable hope and provide a lifeline when nothing seems to make sense.

"The righteous cry out, and the Lord hears them; he delivers them from all their troubles. The Lord is close to the brokenhearted and saves those who are crushed in spirit," wrote King David in Psalm 34:17–18.

And the apostle Paul reminds us that nothing can separate us from the love of Christ.

> Shall trouble or hardship or persecution or famine or nakedness or danger or sword? . . . No, in all these things we are more than conquerors through him who loved us. For I am convinced that neither death nor life, neither angels nor

> demons, neither the present nor the future, nor any powers, neither height nor depth, nor anything else in all creation, will be able to separate us from the love of God that is in Christ Jesus our Lord. (Romans 8:35, 37–39)

God is *always* with us, even through our worst and most tragic days. When we have nothing left, we can cling to Him and know that we don't face anything alone. When we choose to do so, that act of worship glorifies God and sparks new strength within us. It also sets us on a path toward hope, healing, and God's work in and through our pain.

Does that mean we'll get the answers and explanations we want? No. Like Job, we may never know exactly why we have to walk through such hard times. But we can see good sprout and grow in and through us during our pain and problems. We can taste some of God's redemptive power, bringing life out of death in our circumstances just as He is doing and will eventually complete in making His creation right again.

The process helps us grow and become stronger. That's why James encourages us to "consider it pure joy" when we face trials, "because you know that the testing of your faith produces perseverance. Let perseverance finish its work so that you may be mature and complete, not lacking anything" (James 1:2–4).

The concept is the same as that of an athlete who trains his or her muscles to the point of fatigue and weakness so they will heal and grow stronger. As we turn to God, we allow Him to put us back together even stronger, trusting that He is able to bring good out of our worst nightmares (Romans 8:28).

And as God purifies and restores our spirits, we often realize the depths of the brokenness of our humanity. Such a realization fills us with gratitude, grace, and compassion, and it's there that we are able to touch others with the authentic love of Christ. Paul explained it this way: "Praise be to the God and Father of our Lord Jesus Christ, the Father of compassion and the God of all comfort, who comforts us in all our troubles, so that we can comfort those in any trouble with the comfort we ourselves receive from God" (2 Corinthians 1:3–4).

Does that lessen our pain? Not necessarily. But in it, we experience God at work in and through us, restoring and healing. The more we lean into that work, the more we are drawn into worship and shaped by God's presence there. We taste heaven, are drawn to its call, and point to its coming day.

"I don't know how that stuff works, but I do know God can heal," Michael Chislett says after having seen his baby son recover from near death.

"It was a crazy time of life," Matt Crocker says of his sister's death. "It shook our family up, but at the end of the day, it brought us closer together and closer to God. She was the reason I picked up a guitar, so I feel like she's in [Hillsong UNITED] as well, in a weird way." Millions of people around the globe have been touched and encouraged as a result.

"I feel like we're at our best when we're broken because that's the moment when God gets to be made everything," Joel Houston says. "And it gives us an opportunity to love, to trust, and to operate from the place of His strength, not our own."

Such opportunities to see God work in and around us come out of worshiping through our pain.

APPLY

How can we worship through pain?

BE HONEST

Don't be afraid to ask God the hard questions you're feeling. He can handle them. Turn to the book of Psalms for examples. There King David and others poured out their joys and pains. Even Jesus quoted Psalm 22:1 while on the cross: "My God, my God, why have you forsaken me? Why are you so far from saving me, so far from my cries of anguish?" Instead of trying to conceal your hurt, confusion, doubt, anger, or despair from God, pour out those emotions and more to God. Let Him meet you at the end of yourself and carry you far beyond.

DIG DEEP

Worship by diving into the Bible. Sometimes our pain is so great we have no words (Romans 8:26–27). But we can use God's. There is power in God's Word. Reading it, praying it, meditating on it, and clinging to it throughout the day can be the source of hope and comfort that carries us. It can remind us of God's truth and abilities and faithfulness when we have trouble remembering on our own. It is medicine for our hearts.

FOLLOW ONE STEP AT A TIME

Pain knocks us off balance. Grief is a process, filled with ups and downs. Suffering sends us seesawing from hope to despair and back again. But God is with us in every stage. Take His hand, and take the step He offers each day, one at a time. Each trusting step toward Him is an act of worship that realigns our being and reflects glory to the great Healer.

DISCUSS

What is the better question: "Why, God?" or "Why not, God?" Explain your answer.

Is pain the greatest teacher? Why or why not?

Where or how do you rediscover hope in your hard times?

How have you seen God work through pain in your life?

What is your favorite Bible verse for comfort in difficult times?

SING

Worship and sing together. Stream the following song or Google the lyric video.

"OCEANS (WHERE FEET MAY FAIL)"

You call me out upon the waters
The great unknown where feet may fail
And there I find You in the mystery
In oceans deep
My faith will stand

And I will call upon Your name
And keep my eyes above the waves
When oceans rise
My soul will rest in Your embrace
For I am Yours and You are mine

Your grace abounds in deepest waters
Your sovereign hand
Will be my guide
Where feet may fail and fear surrounds me
You've never failed and You won't start now

So I will call upon Your name
And keep my eyes above the waves
When oceans rise
My soul will rest in Your embrace
For I am Yours and You are mine

Spirit, lead me where my trust is without borders

Let me walk upon the waters

Wherever You would call me

Take me deeper than my feet could ever wander

And my faith will be made stronger

In the presence of my Savior

[6x]

Oh, Jesus, You're my God

I will call upon Your name

Keep my eyes above the waves

My soul will rest in Your embrace

I am Yours and You are mine

WEEK 4

WORSHIP THROUGH SERVING

KEY SCRIPTURE

"The King will reply, 'Truly I tell you, whatever you did for one of the least of these brothers and sisters of mine, you did for me.'" —Matthew 25:40

VIDEO CLIP

Watch the clip for week 4, "Worship Through Serving," where Hillsong UNITED serves in Manila, and Joel Houston connects serving to the cross.

STUDY

It's hard to believe people live like that. Getting a firsthand view of extreme poverty can be disturbing and moving. And that's exactly what the members of Hillsong UNITED experienced when they visited the slums of Manila, Philippines, the world's most densely populated city.

There they played with kids and visited homes that are little more than shacks pieced together with scraps and plastic. Water leaks through makeshift roofs. Food is scarce. Children sleep on the floor, and entire families live in single rooms. Each may be a home, but it's hardly a house.

The scene is a far cry from the bright lights and massive arenas where the band often plays, but the motivation to be there is the same.

"Everybody deserves to know that God loves them," Joel Houston says. "It's impossible to truly know Jesus and not have a heart for others, those who are poor and outcast. I pray that will always be the story of our church."

The band visited Manila with Compassion International, a ministry devoted to releasing children from poverty in Jesus's name. It's a natural connection as Hillsong and its members sponsor about 40,000 kids around the world.

"We sing about how much we love God and how much we want to change the world, but you can actually do it," JD Douglass says.

"When you look at the cross, it's got this [vertical] element; then you've got this [horizontal] element where it's reaching out," Joel says. "I love that picture. It starts by knowing God and understanding He loves us personally and then reciprocating by loving God and honoring Him. That's what worship is. If this [vertical] is happening in a way that's honest and real, we're left with no choice but to want to reach out our hands to love others. That's honestly what the Gospel is all about."

JUST LIKE JESUS

Serving other people is an act of worship to God. For the ultimate example, we have no further to look than Jesus Himself. Everything He did was to glorify His Father and to serve others—humans—to the point of laying down His life for us. He came to serve and to sacrifice everything. He said so Himself: "Whoever wants to become great among you must be your servant, and whoever wants to be first must be slave of all. For even the Son of Man did not come to be served, but to serve, and to give his life as a ransom for many" (Mark 10:43–45).

As His followers, we are called to do the same, and to obey that call is to love God by making His priorities our own. Following Jesus means being like Jesus—or becoming more like Jesus as we choose actions that imitate His own. Essentially, it means putting what we say we believe into action. It means turning the love we feel for God into tangible expressions of love for other people. Jesus said that's what will stand out about us to the world: "By this everyone will know that you are my disciples, if you love one another" (John 13:35).

Does that always come easily? No, but that's the point. It's God's supernatural love we are called to live out, so we must rely on the supernatural strength of His Spirit to flow through us. In action, that might look or feel supernatural sometimes—especially related to someone we have a hard time loving—but often it is expressed in ordinary ways.

OTHERS FIRST

We live in a me-first society. We demand our rights. We expect to get the best. We strive to get ahead, often at the expense of others. Most of us have the means and opportunities to make choices based on our wants, likes, and preferences. That's not all bad, but it can draw us into a self-centered and entitled mind-set. God calls us to live in ways that run completely counter to our culture.

The apostle Paul described it well in Galatians 5:13: "You, my brothers and sisters, were called to be free. But do not use your freedom to indulge the flesh; rather, serve one another humbly in love."

Jesus put it simply and clearly when He told His disciples, "Anyone who wants to be first must be the very last, and the servant of all" (Mark 9:35).

Like most spiritual growth, worshiping God through serving others is a self-perpetuating cycle. The more we practice it with our hands, the more it transforms our hearts and becomes a natural part of who we are. Maybe that's why Paul directed the Church to have the same attitude as Jesus:

> In your relationships with one another, have the same mindset as Christ Jesus:
>
> Who, being in very nature God,
> did not consider equality with God something
> to be used to his own advantage;

> rather, he made himself nothing
> by taking the very nature of a servant,
> being made in human likeness.
> And being found in appearance as a man,
> he humbled himself
> by becoming obedient to death—
> even death on a cross! (Philippians 2:5–8)

Did you catch that part about making Himself nothing? Nothing was too lowly for Jesus. That means nothing—or no one—is beneath us when it comes to serving other people.

THE LEAST OF THESE

Our world is filled with extreme socioeconomic disparity. According to statistics cited by Compassion International, almost half of the world—three billion people—lives on less than $2.50 a day. Think about that number. How much did you spend on lunch or your regular coffee today? Can you buy one gallon of gas for your car for that much? What would your life look like if you worked all day every day and earned less than $20 a week?

That's by no means meant to lay a guilt trip on you. It's just a reminder of the reality that we don't usually see first-hand. We certainly have a range of socioeconomic levels in the United States that includes poverty, but we are rich in comparison to most of the world. That's not a bad thing for us; it's an opportunity. Our country has been blessed with great prosperity. How can we use it to bless others, both inside and outside our borders?

Jesus pointed the way:

> Then the King will say to those on his right, "Come, you who are blessed by my Father; take your inheritance, the kingdom prepared for you since the creation of the world. For I was hungry

> and you gave me something to eat, I was thirsty and you gave me something to drink, I was a stranger and you invited me in, I needed clothes and you clothed me, I was sick and you looked after me, I was in prison and you came to visit me."
>
> Then the righteous will answer him, "Lord, when did we see you hungry and feed you, or thirsty and give you something to drink? When did we see you a stranger and invite you in, or needing clothes and clothe you? When did we see you sick or in prison and go to visit you?"
>
> The King will reply, "Truly I tell you, whatever you did for one of the least of these brothers and sisters of mine, you did for me." (Matthew 25:34–40)

Jesus made it clear that He loves and cares for the poor, the oppressed, the lowly, and the outcast—and that He wants us to love and care about them too. Yes, He also loves the prosperous, the beautiful, and the successful. He wants all of us to love and serve each other, and we all have needs no matter what our walk in life is. But it's important for us to remember that Jesus made a special point through His words and actions on earth of reaching out to society's misfits and rejects. Maybe that's because He knew how easy it is for those people to fall through the cracks and be forgotten. He wanted them—and us—to know that God doesn't forget them and neither should we.

Even more important, He wanted us to know that loving God includes loving those people in practical and tangible ways. Later in the Bible, James wrote boldly that "faith by itself, if it is not accompanied by action, is dead" (James 2:17). What kind of actions did he mean? He spelled them out in the preceding verses: meeting the physical needs, including food and clothing, of those who are in need (James 2:14–16). That's challenging. James is basically telling us, "Put up or shut up. If you really believe and follow Jesus, your life should show it."

Looking at the tremendous need in the world can be overwhelming. We might be tempted to think, *Changing the world for billions of people? How am I gonna do that? There's no way. Why even bother?* You're right. That is impossible. That's why our goal and our focus isn't fixing the whole world—it's God Himself, the transformative love of Jesus, and the strength and guidance of the Holy Spirit. As we make ourselves available to God with a servant's attitude, He will open our eyes and show us opportunities all around us to make a difference in one life at a time through one act at a time.

As Joel Houston says on the streets of Manila, "God's not looking for us to do everything. He's just looking for us to do something—usually that's the one thing that's in front of us."

On that day for Hillsong UNITED, it was spending time in Manila and connecting personally with people they and their church serve through Compassion sponsorship. Maybe you'll find yourself with a similar opportunity. Or maybe that something for you is seeing and meeting a need by serving someone who lives literally across the street.

Both are acts of service that worship God, and there are a million more ways all around us.

APPLY

How can we worship through service?

LOOK FOR A NEED, MEET A NEED

Look around you—in your home, your neighborhood, your community. Who needs help? Who is vulnerable? You can bring encouragement, assistance, and hope even through a simple act. Deliver a meal. Mow or rake a yard. Stop and listen. Babysit a kid. Serve a friend, loved one, neighbor, single mom, senior citizen, or stranger. Be creative and reach out generously.

SPONSOR A CHILD

It's an easy way to make a big difference. Compassion International says there are six hundred million children living in poverty around the world. That's a lot, but you can drastically change the life and future of the one you provide an education, nutrition, and the Gospel for. Connect through Compassion International, World Vision, or another ministry and become involved in God's work in the heart and life of a child somewhere around the world.

LEVERAGE YOUR RESOURCES

What kinds of gifts, abilities, and resources do you have? Offer them to a larger ministry around you to magnify your efforts. Start at your church where there are probably many outreach efforts to serve and help different groups of people. Look in your community as well. Maybe you can bring the love of Christ to a service group that's reaching people your church is not. Think globally, and donate to or volunteer with a ministry meeting tangible needs in another country. Ask God for direction, and look for ways to serve people you have a burden for. Remember, you don't have to do everything, but by plugging into a concerted effort with others, your something can go further.

DISCUSS

How does Jesus's call to serve contrast with our culture?

How does serving others convey the Gospel?

Have you had a chance to witness global poverty firsthand? What was your reaction? How did it affect you then and after?

When we reach out to others, who is impacted most?

What one act of service can you commit to doing this week?

SING

Worship and sing together. Stream the following song or Google the lyric video.

"MIGHTY TO SAVE"

Everyone needs compassion
A love that's never failing
Let mercy fall on me

Everyone needs forgiveness
The kindness of a Savior
The hope of nations

Savior, He can move the mountains
My God is mighty to save
He is mighty to save
Forever, author of salvation
He rose and conquered the grave
Jesus conquered the grave

So take me as You find me
All my fears and failures
Fill my life again

I give my life to follow
Everything I believe in
Now I surrender
I surrender

[repeat chorus 2x]

Shine Your light and let the whole world see
We're singing for the glory of the risen King, Jesus
Shine Your light and let the whole world see
We're singing for the glory of the risen King, Jesus

[repeat chorus 2x]

Shine Your light and let the whole world see
We're singing for the glory of the risen King, Jesus
Shine Your light and let the whole world see
We're singing for the glory of the risen King, Jesus
[4x]

WEEK 5

WORSHIP THROUGH SURRENDER

KEY SCRIPTURE

"Father, if you are willing, take this cup from me; yet not my will, but yours be done." —Luke 22:42

VIDEO CLIP

Watch the clip for week 5, "Worship Through Surrender," where Joel Houston struggles with finishing a new song as the band prepares for the Forum concert.

STUDY

The creative process can be difficult. Sometimes inspiration flows, and a song or essay comes together instantly like a gift from above. Other times the blank page looms like a beast, and stringing together a series of words or images is as much of a slog as scaling Mount Everest. The reasons are usually varied and unknown. Why can the process feel so smooth and effortless one time and so weighted and challenging another time?

The members of Hillsong UNITED take their craft seriously. Not only are they committed to musical excellence but they strive for spiritual depth that leads worshipers into the presence of God. As the primary lyricist, Joel Houston especially aims for inspirational metaphor and creative progression. But sometimes the craft is hard to come by.

"It's tricky sometimes, these songs," Joel says. "It's just a process. One minute you think it's awesome; the next it doesn't fit. There might be something in there."

As the band works on a new album in *Hillsong: Let Hope Rise* and prepares to perform at the Forum in Los Angeles, the process is especially difficult to complete. It's one that tests Joel right up to the moment the band takes the stage.

The process is taxing and exhausting. Overall, it is walking a rough path of seeking, trusting, and depending on God. It is a journey of surrender, and each step is an act of worship. Each step leads Joel to a place of remembering and realizing the truths that he passes on to worshipers around the world. As he tells the concert crowd in the film: "No matter what's going on, no matter how big the mountain, how dark the night, how distant God might seem, the truth is that the God of heaven, Creator of the universe, Author of life, He is here, He is with you, He will never fail you."

WAIT ON THE LORD

We don't like to wait. We want what we want, and we want it now. And in most areas of life, we're used to getting it. Our food microwaves in minutes or less. Our information downloads in microseconds. We travel at high speeds. And if we hit any snags or delays, look out: We rage.

We automatically try to apply our normal timetables to our relationship with God. But God's timing works differently. He is more interested in the process of our purification and growth than in our immediate gratification. Worshiping through surrender is a process of adjusting ourselves to His timetable, and often that includes waiting.

The Bible, especially in the Psalms, gives us many reminders to wait on the Lord, such as:

> Wait for the LORD;
> be strong and take heart
> and wait for the LORD. (Psalm 27:14)
>
> I wait for the LORD, my whole being waits,
> and in his word I put my hope.
> I wait for the LORD
> more than watchmen wait for the morning,
> more than watchmen wait for the morning.
> (Psalm 130:5–6)

> Be still before the Lord
> and wait patiently for him;
> do not fret when people succeed in their ways,
> when they carry out their wicked schemes.
> (Psalm 37:7)

But that waiting involves much more than just enduring the passing of time. It means hoping, seeking, offering our desires and needs, expecting, surrendering all of the above to God's care and outcome. That's why the original Hebrew and Greek actually use different words to convey these similar and related aspects of waiting. Our Bible translations often use the word *wait*, but sometimes it varies by translation. The New International Version and New Living Translation use the words *hope* and *trust* in Isaiah 40:31 (respectively), while the New King James Version uses *wait*: "But those who wait on the Lord shall renew their strength; they shall mount up with wings like eagles, they shall run and not be weary, they shall walk and not faint."

We tend to think of waiting as a passive concept. There is an element of patience when it comes to surrendering to God. We willingly give up our control and the manipulation of our circumstances to trust that God can work things out better than we can. But it's also important to remember that surrendering takes an active choice to release control—really, an ongoing series of choices to continue releasing control and to focus on God as the Source of all we need and want.

WALK FAITHFULLY

What do we do while we wait on the Lord? What steps do we take in the process of surrender?

"The only problem is if you just sit there and go, 'All right, God, we're ready,' and wait, wait, wait, wait," Joel says. "No, you've got to do something. You've got to do some work."

The process can seem like a paradox. Sometimes it can mean slowing down or pausing to focus on God or to align with

His timing, but we can't usually press pause on our whole life and the world around us. In reality, the process of surrender is a return to our calling and our Caller as we walk through the steps of our everyday lives.

Abraham is a good example. Throughout his life of faith he faced and chose moments of surrender. When he left his home to obey God's call to a distant land, he surrendered his sense of place and his future (Genesis 12:1–5). God didn't reveal where Abraham was going yet. A passive choice might have been to sit at home and say, "I'm waiting, God. I'm not moving until You tell me where. Please." God didn't reveal that info to Abraham right away. But Abraham had been given the next step, and by taking it, he showed obedience and surrender. He kept moving in the direction God had pointed him. And he demonstrated active waiting on the Lord, stepping out with expectation and hope that God would continue to light the way.

It's the same type of process the band members of Hillsong UNITED take. They apply their musical gifts and abilities toward the direction God has pointed them, and they do so to the best of their ability. They give their best efforts, surrendering them to God and seeking Him expectantly to meet them in the process and guide their work. It's the same process Christians everywhere follow in whatever circles they live: offering their best efforts as they use the gifts God has given them, while at the same time seeking and following God's guidance.

SURRENDER

Surrendering is giving up control and power. It means to stop fighting and to yield. Spiritually speaking, it is opening our hands and hearts and consciously surrendering to God.

We are called to live out surrender in any and all areas of our lives: our relationships, work, finances, interests, ministry, gifts, hobbies, you name it. Surrendering is the worshipful process of realizing and living out the fact that our lives are not our own; they belong to God (1 Corinthians 6:19–20). That's not always easy to do.

Later in his life, Abraham faced what might have been his most difficult moment of surrender when God told him to sacrifice his son, Isaac. Abraham had literally waited on God for decades to fulfill His promise of a son. His love for the boy was undoubtedly immense; he had waited twenty-five years for his son's arrival. And Isaac was a daily reminder of God's faithfulness. God's entire covenant with Abraham seemed to rest on Isaac. Now God was calling for Abraham to give him up.

It was the ultimate act of surrender when Abraham took his only son into the wilderness and placed him on the altar (Genesis 22:1–19). Did he suspect God would come through with a change of plans and an actual lamb when Isaac asked him where the sacrifice was? Was he simply giving an answer to satisfy his observant son? Had God raising Isaac back to life been part of Abraham's wildest dreams? We don't know. But every step toward that mountain and every stone Abraham picked up and stacked were acts of surrender that proclaimed devotion and honor to God. Placing his son on the altar and picking up the knife showed absolute trust in God. Thankfully, God did come through, stopping Abraham and providing a lamb for their sacrifice. You can be sure that moment changed both Abraham's and Isaac's lives forever.

Jesus also lived the path of surrender. His whole mission on earth was a process of fulfilling and surrendering to His Father's will. And it wasn't always easy. "Father, if you are willing, take this cup from me," He prayed, pleading with God to change the plan of His approaching sacrifice and death. But most important are the next words out of Jesus's mouth: "Yet not my will, but yours be done" (Luke 22:42).

Jesus surrendered His will to the Father's. He placed His very life in God's hands. It wasn't the path He would have preferred, but He essentially told God, "I'm all in, no matter what."

We are called to do the same. We can go about our everyday lives serving God in the arenas He has placed us. We can use the gifts He has given us. Even when we don't know what's ahead, we can seek God expectantly, hopefully, and obediently. We can pray, "Not my will, but Yours be done." We can give up control of our very lives and learn to trust God for who He is even more than for what He will give us. We can discover that God meets us as we move toward Him. We can worship through surrender.

APPLY

How can we worship through surrender?

GIVE YOUR LIFE

Surrender begins at the cross. Its origin is responding to God's unfathomable love for you and to Jesus's wide-open arms with your very life. It's an experience of grace and forgiveness. Whether you've never done that before or need a reminder, the experience of giving our lives to Jesus changes us eternally and gives us a foundation of gratitude that drives all our ongoing acts of surrender.

LIVE SACRIFICIALLY

The more we understand God's bigger picture, the easier it is to surrender to Him even when our way seems unclear. Paul encouraged us to offer ourselves as living sacrifices to God and to be transformed as God renews our minds (Romans 12:1–2). It's an ongoing act of worship and surrender. Turning that process into a habit makes life a more natural journey to the beat of God's drum.

LET GO

The moment comes when we simply have to step off the high dive or out of the skydiving plane. We must defy fear with the boldness of action and demonstrate faith by following God's leading. As we seek God, wait for Him, place our hope and expectation in Him, and move forward in faith, we can be confident that He will never leave us or fail us. We belong to Him. We are His work in progress. He will be faithful and true no matter what our circumstances are.

DISCUSS

Where has God placed you? On what path has He pointed your life?

What abilities has He gifted you with that you can use and offer back to His purposes?

What are you waiting for? How is God calling you to wait on Him in the process?

About what do you need to pray, "Not my will, but Yours be done"?

How have you experienced and learned from the process of surrender?

What comes easier to you: fighting or surrendering to God? Why do you think that's true?

SING

Worship and sing together. Stream the following song or Google the lyric video.

"TOUCH THE SKY"

What fortune lies beyond the stars
Those dazzling heights too vast to climb
I got so high to fall so far
But I found heaven as love swept low

My heart beating, my soul breathing
I found my life when I laid it down
Upward falling, spirit soaring
I touch the sky when my knees hit the ground

What treasure waits within Your scars
This gift of freedom gold can't buy
I bought the world and sold my heart
You traded heaven to have me again
My heart beating, my soul breathing
I found my life when I laid it down
Upward falling, spirit soaring
I touch the sky when my knees hit the ground

Find me here at Your feet again
Everything I am, reaching out, I surrender
Come sweep me up in Your love again
And my soul will dance
On the wings of forever
[repeat]

My heart beating, my soul breathing
I found my life when I laid it down
Upward falling, spirit soaring
I touch the sky when my knees hit the ground
[repeat]

Find me here at Your feet again
Everything I am, reaching out, I surrender
Come sweep me up in Your love again
And my soul will dance
On the wings of forever

Upward falling, spirit soaring
I touch the sky
When my knees hit the ground

NOTES